# The Blue Nib
# Chapbook 1

Derek Kannemeyer
Jackie Gorman
Christopher Meehan

Edited by Shirley Bell

The Blue Nib
Chapbook 1

First published in Great Britain in 2018 by The Blue Nib

Copyright © The Blue Nib

The right of Derek Kannemeyer,
Jackie Gorman and Christopher Meehan
to be identified as the authors of this work has been asserted by them in accordance with the
Copyright, Design and Patents Act of 1988

All rights reserved

ISBN: 978-1999955014

# CONTENTS

Introduction ............................................................................................. 1
JUDGE'S REPORT ................................................................................ 2
1st prize: Derek Kannemeyer ............................................................... 3
The Others ............................................................................................ 4
Boat Woman, Towson ........................................................................... 5
Johnny Walks to School with the Wrestler's Kids ............................... 7
Inside the A/C Ducts at American Tobacco ........................................ 9
Ballade on Becoming American ......................................................... 10
Two Flowermen .................................................................................. 11
For the Placeholders .......................................................................... 13
Drapetomania ..................................................................................... 14
Gustave Caillebotte: Floor Strippers, The Artist's Studio .............. 17
2nd prize: Jackie Gorman .................................................................. 19
Photograph of Water .......................................................................... 20
The Blue Hare .................................................................................... 21
The Nest .............................................................................................. 22
Wolves ................................................................................................. 23
Swim .................................................................................................... 24
The Apple Of Your Eye ...................................................................... 25
The Word "No" ................................................................................... 26
Shorn ................................................................................................... 27

3rd prize: Christopher Meehan .......................................................... 28
Abbey Hill in October ...................................................................... 29
Banagher ........................................................................................... 30
Deserted ............................................................................................ 31
Necromancer .................................................................................... 32
Reopening the Mines ..................................................................... 33
The Drying Air ................................................................................. 34
The Ever Changing Definition of Youth in Revolt ........................ 35

## Introduction

Welcome to the Blue Nib's first publication, which showcases the prize-winning entries to our first Chapbook Contest, The Summer/Autumn Chapbook Contest, 2017. The Blue Nib is a not for profit small press and online publishing platform run by editors Shirley Bell & Dave Kavanagh.

In The Blue Nib magazine we offered the 3 winning poets, in first, second and third places, chapbook publication, along with cash prizes and copies of this chapbook. The contest was open to new, emerging and established poets from any country but at least one of the three winners was to be a debutante (with no chapbook or book published previously). In fact, we were delighted to find that all three winners were debutantes, so we are proud to be the first publisher to introduce these new poets into print.

Each entry consisted of 8 poems, in the English language, which were the sole work of the entrant with no translations or 'versions'. The poems could be in verse or prose.

Our judge was the renowned poet Michael Blackburn, who lectures at the University of Lincoln, UK.

We are very pleased to be able to showcase these emerging talents.

Shirley Bell and Dave Kavanagh
The Blue Nib
January 2018
http://magazine.thebluenib.com

# **JUDGE'S REPORT**

There was a reassuring variety of voices and poetic forms in the entries to the competition. Many of the poems dealt with the standard subjects of poetry, ie, close relationships, love, loss, and so on, but others were more adventurous in exploring the experiences of others, or of taking up a different viewpoint from which to look at them. Others deployed a more radical and experimental approach to the writing itself, mingling the playful with the serious.

What makes the winners stand out, and what makes them similar to each other (despite, paradoxically, their great differences) comes down to a number of essential qualities. Each has a confident and distinctive voice. When you read you feel as if you are listening to a real person, and the authority with which they speak encourages you to listen.

Each poet addresses their subject through the presentation of clear and persuasive details, rather than through overt explanations of their feelings.

Each poet has a developed sense of form. That is, whether they employ a self-imposed shape for the poem or appear to let the poem dictate its own stretching out on the page, the poet remains in control and harnesses the power of the words within that shape.

And lastly, the language of each of the winners is economical in its own way. The words are appropriately chosen; they are exact; they are not padding, and they are not allowed to lead the poet on irrelevant byeways. It has been a pleasure to read these entries and refreshing to encounter new, exciting work.

Michael Blackburn

## 1st prize winner:
## Derek Kannemeyer

Derek Kannemeyer is a South African-born, London-raised Richmond, Virginian, whose writing has appeared in publications from *Fiction International* to *Rolling Stone*. His 2017 credits include poems in *Silver Birch Press, Man In The Street, The Wild Word, Sand, Quarterday Review, Stone Bridge Cafe* and *Poetry Virginia Review*.

**The Others**

How much easier to despise you all by kind—
by class, age, sex, race, country. Or the creed you're not: that one
can damn anyone. And it's heady stuff, spokesmouthing
for a God, or a party & its line. But let's keep things small.
Particular. No -*ism*s. Easy gets vulgar.

Not that the biases of anyone
are *ipso facto* a weaponry! Few of us are so vulgar
as to be unkind to those not our kind;

they're just not our people. So what if your manners appall
us? So what if you waste your time in the humanities
or the sciences—at the sportsplex or the cybersuck—smooch small
shrill smelly dogs or big soft rosy bosoms? Does a foible define us?

Except honestly, it is a bit much, isn't it? Your particular kind
of excess? So *non compos mentis*. (Or in the vulgar
tongue, should you prefer that one
belch it for you in plebespeak: it's dumbass. It is wacko.)

In the end, though, one is grateful to you morons, & it is, after all,
your funeral. We thank you, who are so gratifyingly less than us.
For being those we look down on & find small.

**Boat Woman, Towson**

*1. Tadpoles*

The neighbor's girl brings me a jar of tadpoles.
On the bottom is a layer of silt. Above the silt the tadpoles
swim, they are quicker and blacker than the silt, they are black
like ink, writing the history of Asia.
Sir, when I was very small, there was a ditch I played in,
rimmed with banyans and thorn flowers, that filled in the spring
with rain. When I dipped my hands in the mud,
singing, *Come, tadpoles, tadpoles, come,* the tadpoles came,
writing their names in the water… Later,
when the soldiers came, we hid there. We had
carried too much with us from Phnom Penh and we were afraid.
I squinched against the bank, hearing the jeer of orders,
earth over me scuff into dirt… Now I lift
the jar from the hands of the neighbor's girl, and I watch
the silt kick up, the tadpoles dart this way and that, the tadpoles
dive for cover, writing *tadpole, tadpole, tadpole.* I watch them
dive into the kick of silt, the old mud-sack of memories.


*2. Name*

This is how I write my name.
How I wrote it, when I was called it in its language.
Sir, before your ballpoint pen, there was my father's quill—
so quick, like swish-things underwater!
Then slowly and more scratchily, with his hand round mine.
As he guides me across the page, he speaks:
back of each sound he makes, the old called names—
*come, tadpole, come*—come spilling from their sack.
My brother, as he mends his bicycle.
And back of him, the dust the cart wheels kicked up.
Of that, the trees, and roofs jostling the treetops, and streets,
and turns into a map of sidestreets,
to green hills, to a moon of rice-paper.

*3. Bat*

A bat got in my bathroom.
That day, I had received a letter. As I read,
the room my father sat in, lit by one lamp, opened
like an arm. Refolding it, I looked, I saw
this crease of blackness, panting, on a bag of donated blouses;
I took in that it moved; I screamed.
Sir, what did I think I was fighting, where did
the darkness come from, was it back, or out, or in?
When it was almost dead, I thrust it in the bowl.
It would not flush. It lay panting and I wept.
What did I think I was killing?
My neighbor saved me. When I came back to,
my wrists clasped in her hands, I could feel her feel
the fight go out of them. She let them loose.
She slipped her fingers through my fingers. So gently…
But sir, her husband. Looked at me. As if
I were a piece of blackness. He had just seen move.


*4. Tadpoles*

Now their daughter brings me tadpoles.
All day, I am a girl again!
I watch them chart the spirals of the jar, and write
my name, and wait for them to turn to something else.
Sir, translate it for me, this figure for trapped things,
from this my alphabet, whose twists
reroute me to lost cities, from this my own sweet tongue,
whose jar of dark syllables
for me alone throws edges, shadows, light.

**Johnny Walks to School with the Wrestler's Kids**

I walk to school with the wrestler's kids.
They walk like grown-ups, smooth and spare.
They look at the world through hooded lids.
They look at me like I'm hardly there.

I wait for them by the EXXON sign.
*My dad's a teacher. He calls me Jack.*
*We're new in town, I like it fine.*
I talk to them but they don't talk back.

Patrick is seven. I'm almost seven.
George is ten. He smells, a bit.
Kevin's thirteen. He's big, is Kevin.
He sets the pace. We keep to it.

But sometimes Thursday, sometimes Friday,
across the pedestrian overpass,
between the slip road and the highway,
Patrick topples me to the grass—

locking his elbow around my neck—
pinning me between earth and sky…
If I wiggle free, George turns me back.
Kevin stands watching the cars go by.

I walk to school with the wrestler's boys.
I sing and kick tin-cans. They call me the Noise.
They say my name like they're spitting phlegm.
Sometimes, I walk like I'm one of them.

We're wrestler's boys; we're lean and cool;
we don't need you and we don't need school.
Sometimes I walk like I'm big and tough.
When my teacher winks, I start to laugh.

She winks at me, as if they don't count.
They look at the world through their hooded lids.
Blankly ahead, as if maybe they don't.
I walk to school with the wrestler's kids.

**Inside the A/C Ducts at American Tobacco**

It's light enough in here to read the label on the whiskey bottle
Buck swigs or seems to swig from and swings back to Leon;
light enough to read Buck's face and know he's being polite,
that at his age he's a little scared of Leon; would rather do
the work we're up here sweltering to get done—scraping from
the duct walls their crustcoats of tobacco smell—and haul ass
down; but thinking back, where can the light have come from?
Around us, the pipes are dull 0's going nowhere, and Leon
is kneeling on the one shut trapdoor out... I'm younger then,
fresh out of grad school and sightseeing the work world: office
temping, some light industrial, worse comes to worst, a visit to
the tip of the dark continent of retail. Industrial's best. Most alien,
most separate from who I am. Leon scrapes one-handed, drunk,
with more brisk, vigorous efficiency than me both-fisted sober,
like someone nonchalantly, fiercely masturbating, who hasn't
noticed he's been at it five hours straight. *The way I see it*, he's
telling Buck, *I'm a king, I got a right to all them women. My wife,
though, I catch her messing around one time, that bitch is done,
my obligation's over. Now you talking*, Buck chimes in sometimes,
though Leon barely, in fact, shuts up. *Amen, brother. Got dat right.*
There's light from somewhere to see the sweat on him, to gauge
the tight disclaimer of his smile: *I'm just appeasing Mr. Crazy!*
His scraper arm, in shadow, climbs the shaft. Mine's a side panel.
Leon has the floor, working the jerky tom-tom of our busy signal.
We rasp and peel. Each archback of stripped skin releases a sweet
toxic stink, so omnipresent I can't smell it till I'm miles away,
heaving my work clothes off in volleys, to step over their ripe
sprawl like a body. Figure of death or dissolution, there's not light
enough to tell; *whichever of them bitches wants me baddest.*

## Ballade on Becoming American

> "The nail that sticks out will be hammered down"
> Asian proverb

Song Li, in the new shirt that doesn't fit
he picked out from the box the church group gave—
my uncle's eyes, sharp, slant, and obdurate—
leans forward as the maintenance foreman, *Dave,*
instructs him how the yoking pins behave.
Song Li, who can't yoke English verb to noun,
nods once, and points behind the autoclave.
A bolt that's worked loose must be hammered down.

The job proves simple; what he strains to get
are the talk radio voices, wave on wave.
But learns by heart the jingles, bit by bit
slotting the nonsense sounds into their stave:
sings, as he showers, of Electrashave—
recalling oceans where he didn't drown,
through knowing where to trim, and what to save;
how nails that stick out must be hammered down.

Broad corporate lawns, greenly immaculate,
unroll for him, for he is free and brave.
After night school, he's at his TV set,
compiling lists of what the neighbors crave.
He has us pegged—the liberal guilt enclave.
His sponsor drives a Beetle, rusted brown;
is asked to park it one street back, and shave.
The nail that sticks out will be hammered down.

Until, Song Li, sore thumbs are all we have
to snag what's left of Kampot, of Cape Town.
I sing your children's burden, no less grave:
how different trees might lean from common ground.

**Two Flowermen**

I often found something courteous to say
to the flowerman. Once or twice, anyway?
His flowers, the loveliness of the day.

On a corner of Grove and Boulevard,
spring through summer, backstopped by a courtyard
of flowerless shrubs and low clumps of sward,

he set out his Sunday stall. Blooms galore!
Him less colorful. Fiftyish. White, poor,
rural. No hat to tip; but the look he wore—

the briskly bobbed head, the smile dimpling
into a simper, then gone—said the thing.
(You know what supplicant, subservient thing.)

Then one June Sunday, as I ambled by
with my *Times* and my croissants, a thin cry
stopped me: *Sir!* I turned. Arch-browed, stern of eye.

He had to, like, *go*. Would I be so good
as to man his stand? *Me?* Well, fun! I would!
A church bell pealed. I stood where he had stood—

working my patch, a fellow rich in flowers—
as he lunged scrunch-limbed down the road. For hours,
reader—well, more than half one—I sold flowers—

me!—from my turf on Boulevard and Grove—
a shoehorned-in but redolent alcove—
to old coots, gruff matrons, couples in love

with their June selves—as I was, by the way!
And some folks found a word or two to say
as they swished by: my flowers; the pretty day.

Proudly, he bid me keep the change I'd earned,
My flowerman: not much. Still, you'll have discerned
it quietly jangling a few lines I've turned.

**For the Placeholders**

>"A significant zero in the decimal representation of a number."
>The Apple Dictionary

>"In the decimal form of a number, a digit that is not significant."
>The Free Online Dictionary

For the stand-ins; for the almosts.
For that woman whose name you can't recall, willing to do *whatever
or whoever it took*... Who after it took the not enough she had,
took one, two, took 300 for the team (who were everyone else:
exclude no one, whether they know you exist or not).

For the significant zeros (or the insignificants? whatever)—
in their quiet way they make (or not)
a difference: let's join to declare them who we count on most.

For that hero, the common man; the kitchen wench; the Santa's elfs—
yea, in their ridiculous numbers, the brave little people—
who are us, mostly; but better to think of them as someone else.
And for the small ways they battle to fill this space that bounds them,

to become these very almosts. Listen, almost
is hard. But it's about the order we bring to our lives, or not—
how we draw our in/out lines, demarcating a canon: because whatever
casts out, defines. (Whose cost is that what defines, casts out.)

So for the grunts, runts, once coulds. The strays, the good grey gestalts.
These selves that we settle for by not being something, someone.
For the ways we settle for being someone else.

**Drapetomania**

> "[What] induces the negro to run away from service is as much a disease of the mind as any other species of mental alienation, and much more curable, as a general rule."
> Samuel A Cartwright, "Report on the Diseases and Physical Peculiarities of the Negro Race," 1851.


1.
There's a name for this madness, the madness of the runaway slave—
and as I guessed instinctively, it is curable. So that
when they brought James back to us, I set about curing it.


At the treatment center they taught me the name, *drapetomania*,
and once we were checked in, I showed it to James in his file—
just the shape of the letters, at that time, of course—
in the Rehabilitation Lounge, they called it, side by side on its flowered
                                                                          sofa,
as the TV played a sports show. And out of the doctor's hearing, I gave
                                                                          my word,
I swore it by my love for him, that one day he'd learn to read and write
                                                                                       it,
this word or any he might wish. The law of it be damned, I'd grant him
                                                                        that power.


He was saying little back just yet. But I was not discouraged. I would
                                                                        remain patient.


I laid my hand on the slump of his shoulder and repeated the promise; I
                                                                       unlocked
his manacles and thrust them in my pocket; and turning at the door, I
                                                                       said, *No more*.

He looked up then—perhaps he was remembering when we were boys,
and my father was master, who let the house slaves' kids and us play
                                                  with, as friends—
he looked and the line of his mouth tightened, fighting off the moment
                                                  I saw was coming;
so that I murmured, *Get well, James*, and rapped for the guard to release
                                                          me—
to afford him the dignity of his privacy. So that he might weep, if weep
                                                  he must, alone.


And although as I clicked the door shut I could hear him, his sobs begun,
I would not linger there or eavesdrop, but moved firmly along the hall,
and out into the car park, to drive away, and let them do their work.


2.
They did it well; James came back to us and served us faithfully,
fifteen more years; and if at first his story seems honorable but
                                                  unremarkable—
for he was one of the world's legion of honorable, ordinary men—
yet what an extraordinary legacy, in the end, he left us.


Because I kept my promise. James learned his letters.
And then I and a few like me fought to eradicate the laws that forbade
                                                       this thing,
until—in James's name—we won all slaves the privilege of literacy,
and every master who wishes it the right to teach it. So that this very
                                                    book I hold
is one which at his death James owned—to keep by his cot, and mark in
                                                    the margins of.

There was also a copy book we worked on, and I have given my
                                            permission
that his daughter retain possession of that, and of his Bible—
on the flyleaf of which there is a prayer he wrote, of thanks, which he
                                            recited to me—
and made me in his hand a copy of—which, in a moment, I will share
                                            with you…
What else he wrote, the diaries and the library marginalia, I have not
                                            read;
they are no one's business. The diaries I have ordered burned; his books,
                                            we bury with him.


3.
I have come to believe there are mysteries in this life we do better not to
                                            penetrate.
I do not understand what brought my friend James—yes, I will name him
                                            *friend*—
to the madness that caused him, once, to run from me—but I do not need,
I think, to understand it. Is it not enough that it passed, and that it brought
                                            us closer?
Is it not enough to be grateful for our blessings, and to thank God for all
                                            He has given us?
For what James, in the prayer he wrote and gave to me, this prayer, calls:


*The seven yellows of the sun, for which we thank you, Lord*
*The nine blues of the changing sky, for which we thank you, Lord*
*The thirteen gingers of the hearth-fire, for which, Lord, we thank you*
*The twenty greens of tree, leaf, stalk, stem, blade, for which we thank you*
*The single dark that falls on all of us, that has no hue or name but yours,*
*Lord, for which we wait, in hopes one day to thank you.*

## Gustave Caillebotte: Floor Strippers, The Artist's Studio

> Caillebotte presented *Raboteurs de parquet* at the 1875
> Salon. The jury, no doubt shocked by its raw realism,
> rejected it, some critics talking of "vulgar subject matter."
> Adapted from an article on the Musée D'Orsay website

Three floor sanders: stripping his stained wood's glow
back to a natural light. They lean into

the strain of it, dug-kneed on lacquered boards—
dark strips, striped with light, that bear them onwards

like the grooves of tracks. They ride the task of it,
their bare backs arched to take the lash of light,

their stripped torsos buff as the naked wood,
set on their stage as though choreographed: heads

of slick dark hair identical; same pants,
skin, and pose: of hard muscle held, made dance.

The flourishes, though, are a stubborn mess:
fat tatters of shavings; a bottle, a glass;

two work bags in the corner a slung smudge.
Too vulgar for high art, most critics judged.

Which may dumbfound us now. The beauty we
once had to strain, against good taste, to see.

Behind us, Caillebotte's window, its spare skyline.
Before us, our page; our task of bearing down.

## 2nd Prize Winner:
## Jackie Gorman

Jackie Gorman is from Athlone, Ireland. Her poetry has been published in the following journals ; *Poetry Ireland Review, The Lonely Crowd, Wordlegs, The Lakeview International Review of Arts & Literature, The Honest Ulsterman, The Galway Review, Headspace, Bare Hands, The Sentinel Literary Quarterly, Tales From The Forest, Sow's Ear Poetry Review* and *Obsessed With Pipework*. She has been long-listed for the Erbaccae Poetry Prize, the Allingham Poetry Prize, the Dermot Healy International Poetry Award and the Africa Day Poetry Award. She has been commended in the Goldsmith International Poetry Competition and the Patrick Kavanagh Poetry Awards. She has won the Phizzfest Poetry Award and the Single Poem Award at Listowel Writers Week. She had a poem highly commended in the Poem of the Year Award at the Bord Gais Irish Book Awards in 2017. She is currently studying for an MA in Poetry Studies at the Irish Centre for Poetry Studies at Dublin City University and is part of Poetry Ireland's 2017 Introductions Series, which profiles and supports emerging poets in Ireland.

**Photograph of Water**

The photo was taken the evening I drowned.
I am in the water just below the surface.
The lake is in a deep slumber
not woken by the pike
as it trembles through its dreams.
The rats sleep near the edge,
dreaming of ripe fruit and milk.
I cannot say how old I am
as the water and light plays tricks.
Look long enough and you will see me floating.

**The Blue Hare**

Stepping off the path,
a silver car rushes by.
I never saw it coming,
yet I felt the ground give way.
I knelt down within myself.

The hare that lives in my mind,
snug in her thick coat and
safe in her wide-open eyes,
breaks free and runs across me.

She purrs, sniffs my body,
looks up, pisses and moves on.
So it happens that I am reborn
into my warm russet fur and strong legs.

Mountain hare, white hare,
Irish hare, blue hare.
Many names, one thumping spirit.

A hare will not move until it has to,
stillness and camouflage its defence,
safe in its form of flattened earth.
What does it mean to be free ?
Hare breath touching the ribs.
Watching everything going still,
galloping through swirls of thyme,
sedge and gorse.

**The Nest**

Among the mud and twigs, I saw my father's death.
There was grey hair, a walnut cardigan button,
a black pen and a brain haemorrhage.
A clot, the colour of a fire engine.
Cow parsley drowned in the clogged capillaries.
Shock, cold and indigo in colour,
bound to the heart.
The perfumed stench of impermanence
hung over the forget-me-nots.
A nervous bird with a red pointed beak.
The moorhen lingered near our house,
at the water's sunlit edge.

**Wolves**

I heard the rough magic of a wolf howl.
In our soft den in the Ore Mountains,
I listened as they circled outside.
Shades of white, ochre and umber,
long silver muzzles and flaxen eyes.
Baying sounds from biblical times,
the rapacious spoilers of innocence.
I felt them snuffling at our door and
I heard their low lonely whines.
You said the wolves wouldn't show themselves,
unless they were trying to tell us something.
I quivered and heard myself make
unfamiliar sounds that rendered us apart.

I thought of a winter long ago,
your hands warm as fur.
My bloody heart, thrown to the wolves,
wailing loudly through the fresh blue snow.

**Swim**

I am watching a man swim,
his front crawl throwing light.
His body, shining in the lake shadows,

his hair tangled like wet rushes.
He does not seem to breathe.
A blackbird flies across the stones.
For a moment, my mind wanders
and I watch him in a day-dream.
Skin dripping and smelling of the lake,
he will take my car and drive home.

I will sit here on the shore and wait.
There will be a slow steady breeze
blowing in from the woods.
The sound of the tapping waves
will seem hurried and tactile,
like a baby at the breast.
When my mother answers the door,
she will see this intrepid man
with bits of sunlight shimmering in his hair.

She will see the blackbird dancing in his eyes.
She will watch his open mouth incapable of speech.
Her mouth may open as if she's about to talk,
but maybe my saying so is just a faint hope.
And I, having exchanged with him,
will swim away, into the waters,
out of reach.

**The Apple Of Your Eye**

I am an apple, waiting to hit the ground,
not wanting to be damaged or bruised.
Fragrant and fragile, you could probably smell
the stench of need from the street.
You strolled into the orchard one day
and you picked me, the sinuous tug of wanting.

I keep asking you to wash the stain
from your hand but it's impossible.
How could you keep it clean,
when you hold a whole heart
between your fingers ?

Sometimes, you hear a whimper or a yelp.
Each sound unique,
with as many whorls as a fingerprint.
The truth of things falls like snow,
silently and softly into your life.

**The Word "No"**

Using the word "no" needs some rehearsal,
groaning it silently into mirrors.
Making the shape of it with your mouth,
a poisoned heart-felt kiss.
Learning it in different languages,
sensuous and salty,
rolling off the tongue like a wet oyster.

When I see the sunlight, I will forget Icarus.
I will fly as close to the sun as I want to.
I will sing your name and the word "no".
I will see my feathers and the waves,
yet I will not curse my curious artistry.

**Shorn**

Pale blue eyes looking up,
I put nitroglycerin under your tongue,
as we watch the football and hum "Nessum Dorma".
I help you to shave or tie a Windsor Knot,
each time noticing the beige circle on your cheek,
melanoma erased by radiotherapy.

In July, you planted a rosemary bush.
Covered in ancient toil and sweat,
I help you undress in the hallway.
Closing the bathroom door, seeing you naked,
all of you was vulnerable and shorn.
Shivering like a cold lamb.
My skin burnt silently and slowly.

You looked at me awkwardly.
I write you a poem with naked eyes.

## 3rd prize winner:
## Christopher Meehan

Christopher Meehan lives in County Galway, Ireland. In 2012 he was shortlisted for the Fish International Poetry Prize while in 2013 he was placed 3rd in the Over-The Edge New Writer of the Year Competition. His poems have been published in *Skylight 47, Boyne Berries, Crannog* and *Ropes*.

**Abbey Hill in October**

Evelyn, I followed the ghost of a flying column*
down off the Carran plateau – the brave sons of farmers,
now marching on an enemy long disappeared.
Through hills that once rang out with dirty rhymes
about the queen; these men no longer sang,
their mouths omitting only the star strung hinge
of a redwing, in a call that refuses to be parted from night.

And you were there in the haws, the well,
the distant curve of the Martello tower,
running colours that hold the eye for just long enough
to know, that everything we ever needed is here,
wrapped in an autumn where a breath in chill
clings to limestone, like the curling smoke of October
fires above the cold wet roofs of New Quay.

In an ending to turn me homeward;
twisting shorebirds carved wild petroglyphs
into the sienna of evening, while in through their chanting,
voices drifted up from the haunted fields of Corcomroe.
Signs that there would be no bloodshed, just the
marching of winter thrushes in a brigade of rusted wings,
their single notes rising, in perfect pitch to the Pleiades,

before dropping down into a valley of silence.

*The name given to small groups of fast moving Irish rebels during their guerrilla war
(1919-1921) with occupying English forces.*

**Banagher**

Before we called her mother, she was here,
I can still feel the wind from the all encompassing
Sweep of her dreams as they drift off the river
And settle by the Callows in a silent convergence of wings.
Drawn to the light of a creative mind,
To the unkempt borders of a heart gone to seed;
They would arise and journey in a flock of visions
To where she waited, net in hand, to capture
Those fleeting forms, to measure their hope,
To weigh their promise before tagging and freeing,
In an endless cycle of catch and release.

As they beat against the windows of a midland night,
I wonder at the strength it took to follow their migration,
To ensure their safe passage, so that one Summer
They would return for me, emerging from above the acres
Of meadowsweet where once the rasps of a Corncrake
Sealed the ancient covenant between bird and sky.

**Deserted**

On the cross where
O' Curry Lane meets main street,
he lies, crucifixion complete,
on the winter tarmacadam.

In his proof of
our village aloneness
half an hour was the
record to beat.

For forty minutes;
no trucks, no cars,
no vans, no buses,
until a Ford forces

a hasty resurrection
and a road home
To a brother -
Who is making for Perth.

**Necromancer**

Holding court north of Moher,
A path beaten through rock and bramble,
A henge of upright solids,
The picture will show a giant boulder,
There is warmth through a cup in cold hands,
A slow passing shower,
You, me and the farmers dog watched night –
That lunar necromancer,
Pull the moon up from the brow of the islands,
As the sun fell away from the curvature of the earth.

**Reopening the Mines**

The town feels like Friday,
He drifts through the farmer's market,
Face paler than a bleached moon,
A dancing waif, side-stepping the baby
Hugging mothers and fathers buying organic
In their brightly coloured knits.

This in a week of protracted silence,
Of lights going out on the second knock,
Of a shadow fitting a loose description
Seen snorkelling in a sea of roses
On the square, after the scotch
Had met the night and so completely.

Two years since the cave-in,
Since hope crumbled leaving nothing
To buttress the light against the creeping
Darkness of November, and yet still they wait
For him daily, throwing their words over the side
Until the tunnels and collapsed chambers

Are coated in brightly hued clichés
Around time healing and things picking up.
To be trapped down there where it hurts,
Where once he dug out the good stuff from
The Pyrite of the past and then hear them talking
Of reopening the mines, when all he

Longs for is time, an air pocket to inhabit
Between the inhalation and the piercing screams.

**The Drying Air**

Tomorrow, the home help
Will hover over him,
Her shadow flitting like
A migrant butterfly
Out on the flirting buddleia.

Removing the bandage,
She'll scold him for not having
Faith in the healing power
Of the drying air, never knowing
Of the prayer he carried

To the west-sloping peat lands,
Where face wet from the salt-laden
Drizzle, he laid altars of
Turf at the feet of the
Failing sun.

**The Ever Changing Definition of Youth in Revolt**

I used to think it meant ditching school for drinking
or wrapping a Subaru around a pole at midnight
out of your head on pills, until they flew them into Galway,
nineteen, twenty and twenty three, laid out
in a private clinic, on their hands the blood shed
for the liberation of Libya, in their nightmares,
their neighbour's boy, his face burnt red from the licking flames
and no longer from the shame that came when his mother
would call him 'petal'. Then it got darker.

It was the end of April, I drove out to the valley
behind Ballybornagh to escape the newsfeed
as they hunted a violent but misguided child
through the suburbs of Boston. Minutes before they cheered
at his half-dead eyes, I smothered the imagined gunshots
with the double barrelled repertoire of a Cuckoo,
and this just in…

**The Perfect Height**

When the winter drops something bitter into the wind,
the charm of hail spat by that ripping gale will look
for any opening, hunting the pulse that I live for,
that sits between your neck and a scarf bought for Christmas.

On the back avenue of Woodlawn demesne,
I would draw you in - close, my back to it, the perfect height
to rest my chin on the top of your head, until this warmth,
invisible, has shaken off the cold of a hard migration,

the distance falling from us, as the red Saharan dust might,
from the wings of a Swallow onto the floor of our leaking shed.

www.ingramcontent.com/pod-product-compliance
Lightning Source LLC
Chambersburg PA
CBHW061310040426
42444CB00010B/2578